CRACKERS
& Crumbs

crackers and crumbs
crackers and crumbs
these are my fingers
these are my thumbs
these are my eyes
these are my ears
they'll all grow big
in the next few years

CHANTS FOR WHOLE LANGUAGE

CRACKERS
& Crumbs

Sonja Dunn
with Lou Pamenter

HEINEMANN
Portsmouth, NH

Pembroke Publishers Limited
528 Hood Road
Markham Ontario L3R 3K9

Canadian Cataloguing in Publication Data
Dunn, Sonja, 1931-
  Crackers and Crumbs

ISBN 0-921217-44-7

1. Chants. 2. Music in education. I. Pamenter,
Lou. II. Title.

GV1215.D87 1990   398.8   C90-093199-X

Published in the U.S.A. by
Heinemann Educational Books, Inc.
70 Court Street
Portsmouth, NH 03801

Library of Congress Cataloging-in-Publication Data
Dunn, Sonja.
  Crackers and crumbs: chants for whole language/Sonja Dunn with
Lou Pamenter.
     p.   cm.
  ISBN 0-435-08528-X
  1. Education, Preschool — Activity programs. 2. Language
experience approach in education.   I. Pamenter, Lou.   II. Title.
LB1140.35.C74D86   1990
372.6—dc20   89-78077
                                                     CIP

Cover design by John Zehethofer
Cover photography by Ajay Photographics.
Typesetting by Jay Tee Graphics Ltd.

Printed and bound in Canada by Webcom Limited
0 9 8 7 6 5 4 3 2 1

Acknowledgments

I would like to say thank you to a very supportive family: my husband Bill, my sons Paul and Kevin, daughters-in-law Deborah and Lisa, and my inspiring grandchildren, Brian and Kaitlin.

I have appreciated the support given by fellow members of the Canadian Society of Canadian Authors, Illustrators, and Performers, the Writers' Union of Canada, and the League of Canadian Poets. In particular, I have enjoyed the encouragement of the CANSCAIP writers' workshop.

Thanks to all my faithful friends and relatives who believe in what I am doing. A special thank you to the many children and educators who have enjoyed my chanting, and who, in turn, have given me ideas for more chants.

As well, my thanks to Lou Pamenter for putting together all my ramblings into the helpful notes for educators and care-givers.

The music for ''A Capella'' was developed by me, and the music for ''Push Button Baby'' was developed by Paul Dunn. Our thanks to Nancy Reynolds, Toronto singer and voice teacher, for transcribing this music.

I am pleased to be able to include the following chants, the copyrights for which are held by Paul Dunn: ''Feed the baby'', ''Popsicles'', ''Push Button Baby'', ''Chantski''.

John Zehethofer must be thanked for his attractive book design, and David Prothero for his delightful illustrations.

Sonja Dunn

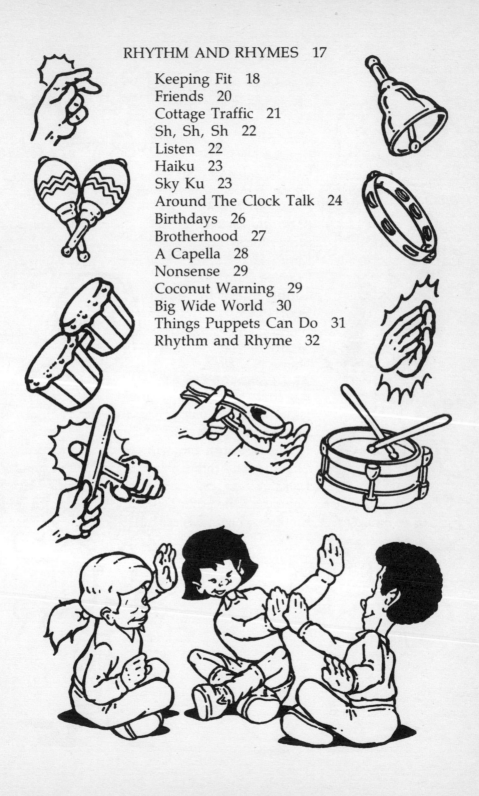

RHYTHM AND RHYMES 17

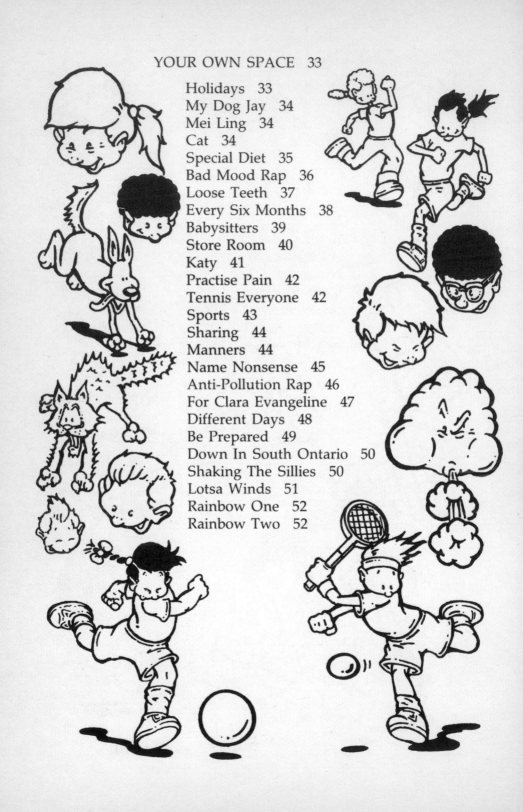

YOUR OWN SPACE 33

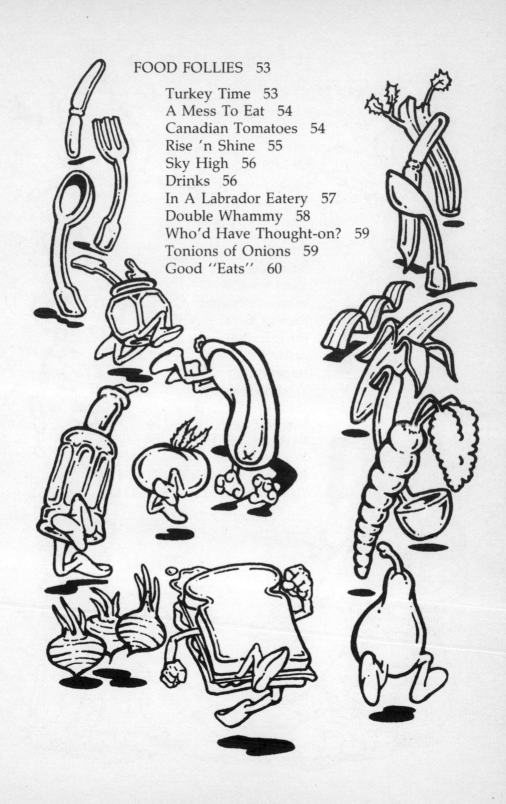

FOOD FOLLIES 53

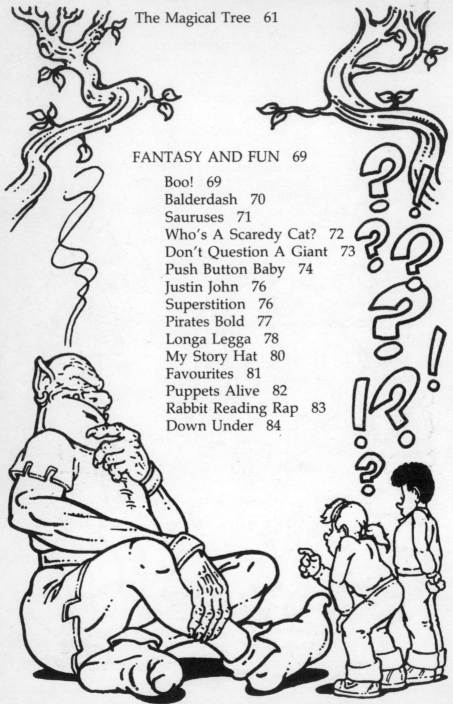

SPECIAL TIMES 85

PLACES TO BE 91

Introduction

Playing with language, discovering ownership of language, experimenting with language is what working with chants is all about. Learning experiences should be inter-disciplinary, integrated experiences. Chants can provide a strategy that develops *reading skills*, ease in *dramatic situations*, sidebars in *art work*, *communication* abilities, *awareness of self and environment*, and skills in *cooperation*. Chants are a workshop in whole language.

Reading skills: children need to explore words, ideas, roles, and emotions; this they can do through reading. Reading is really an act of participation. Chants encourage participation because they are so accessible. The rhythm and rhyme are understood almost immediately. The topics of chants are centred around what children know and love. Through reading chants, children understand more words, and begin to use them more effectively because they have been learned in a setting to which they relate.

Dramatic situations: chants often have an intrinsic dramatic possibility. Children learn how to improvise a dramatic accompaniment to the words; they discover that they should whisper, shout, or sing, depending on the words. They can mime actions to words. They can add new words, possibly learning how to extend dialogue. Through working with a chant, children learn that they can bring new meaning to words — language can be enhanced. Dance, costume, and music can all be added to chants, adding new dimensions to the "expressions" children can make. Tableaux or "frozen pictures" can often be used to illustrate the theme of a chant. Children are satisfied with these dramatic extensions.

Art work: chants extend into art work of several types. Simple drawing may be done to illustrate a chant's content. Several drawings may be needed to describe the content of a longer chant. This could even lead to a "roller show" of images, if the chant had several "scenes". This means that drawings could be attached to each other in sequence and then the ends attached to sticks. The story would unfurl simultaneously with an oral presentation of the chart. Puppets could be made that would present certain chants to a group. Puppets can be as simple as a work sock and as complicated as one with defined features and costumes (although simple materials can still be used). Collages, collections of chants with accompanying drawings, papier-mâché, three-dimensional sets are all possible chant extensions.

Communication abilities: a goal of reading, the learning of communication skills and processes can be gained from working with chants. Chants can be done in groups, making it easier for individuals to participate. The words can be presented through actions or mime. Chants often have repetition within them which allows children to feel an ownership of those words, and delivering them becomes much less difficult. Without much conscious thought, children find that they are communicating clearly, showing their emotions, sharing ideas with others.

Awareness of self and environment: chants talk about children's immediate environments as well as their imaginative parts. The language ''speaks'' to them, and they respond with stories and chants of their own. Discussions can follow on topics such as pollution, family, pets, what frightens them, health, friends, cross-cultures, and science.

Cooperation: a chant is a shared experience. No matter how large the group, everyone has to work together to find the appropriate cadence and movement for the chant. Shared, interactive experiences promote active, participating readers who will improve their skills as they go along. Shared experiences often lead to mutual respect and an interest in experimentation. Since chants offer possibilities in reading, acting, choreography, music, and art, children can cooperate in an interest group that suits them.

No matter how you interact with children — as a parent, teacher, librarian, friend — you are the mediator between the ''story'' and the child. Your enjoyment of the chants will translate itself to the children. If you are using the chants in a remedial situation or with children of different abilities or with children who have English as a second language, reading the chants aloud yourself is a first step. Chants with some repetition are good openers because the children feel they can join in more easily. The words can be written down in a large book format so that children can see the words as they hear them. Overhead transparencies also work well for those children who have limited reading ability. If you use a flipboard or chalkboard to show the words, and you want different groups to say different lines, those lines can be written in a different colour; the concept chunks are then easier to visualize.

It's true that, with you as a facilitator, chants and children can springboard into many other disciplines. But, good chants are fundamentally full of rhythm and rhyme — and are fun. They can be fun because of their word-play, because of their imagery, because of their shape, but good chants should delight. If that delight translates into something more, well, that's great.

Children are secrets.
Don't tell their surprise.
To see magic visions
Just look through their eyes.

You will be able to use some of the chants in *Crackers & Crumbs* to enhance stories you tell, to create cooperative chants and raps, to introduce specific areas, to participate in the whole language approach. But, more than anything else — enjoy chanting. You will find it can be entertaining, involving, instructional, satisfying, and fun.

Can't stop
Chanting
Raving
Ranting

Rapping
Bopping
Dubbing
Toasting
Cheering
Rocking
Rolling
Roasting

Yell some words
that make you dance
That's the way
you make your chants.

Sonja Dunn
Lou Pamenter

15

Rhythm and Rhyme

The two fundamental elements in chants are rhythm and rhyme. They can be obvious elements or they can be elements that have to be uncovered, played with, and worked on to find the right pitch.

Rhythm is best understood as a "beat" in music. The beat of a chant can be slow and stately which will give the words a serious, maybe even sombre cast. Or the slowness can simply be the imitation of movement that is characteristic of a character or time described in the chant. The rhythm of a chant can be extremely quick, almost skipping in quality. Such a beat could indicate a jolly, happy feeling. Sometimes, a chant can combine several rhythms to show some change or progress in the narrative. Understanding the rhythms of a chant adds to the comprehension of the text.

Rhyme concerns the repetition of sounds. These sounds can be repeated just once, twice, many times, or appear within words rather than at the ends. The inherent musical quality in rhymes is understood by children quite easily, enabling them to respond quickly to new sets of words. Children have a natural affinity for rhythm and rhyme.

Keeping Fit

Mike Mike
Ride that bike

Rose Rose
Kiss your toes

Joe Joe
Start to row

Jack Jack
Run the track

Di Di
Touch the sky

Peg Peg
Shake a leg

Paul Paul
Kick the ball

Jim Jim
Get in the swim

Kate Kate
Swirl and skate

Ann Marie
You'd better ski

Dennis Dennis
Play some tennis.

Make a hit
By keeping fit!

Keeping Fit illustrates a basic rhyme and simple rhythm. Its simplicity makes it a very accessible chant, moving along in easy rolls of sounds. Yet its simplicity allows for a great deal of creativity. Children will enjoy making up their own rhyming lines. They can add to this chant, staying with the theme of physical fitness or they can tackle another theme, using their own names for rhymes. Actions can accompany each pair of lines, done by the class as a whole or taken by individuals. The action verbs will lead naturally to physical involvement.

Pantomimes of different exercises or activities can allow others to guess the activity, and then find an appropriate rhyme for it. Using this chant or additional ones created by the children is an ideal way to re-inforce the information in a teaching unit on the need to maintain a healthy level of personal fitness.

Friends

Are you French
Are you Dutch
Are you Macedonian
Or British
Or Greek
Or Patagonian?
Maybe you're Irish
Or Welsh
Or Iranian
Polish
Or Yiddish
Perhaps you're Ukrainian.
Italian or Polish
Perchance you're American
African
Mexican
Native Canadian
You could be Chinese
Pakistani
Or Asian.

Lebanese
Portuguese
Wherever will it end?

No matter what you are
You'll always be my friend!

There are rhythm changes within *Friends*. Children will have to play with the words until they find a way of reading each of the lines that suits them.

Cottage Traffic

Driving
From the cottage
Late at night
See a looooong
Red
Tail
Of lights
Slow as a snail
Bumper to bumper to bumper to bumper
Grownups say it's a bore
I love watching
This red
      S
        N
          A   K   E.

Children can develop their own rhythm for a chant like *Cottage Traffic*. A chorus of ''bumper to bumper to bumper to bumper'' can provide a cohesive background sound. This chant is good for dramatization, finishing with a group slithering around the room like a long red snake. Based on a concrete situation that most children will have experienced, being part of a long line of traffic after dark, this chant can lead to imaginative re-tellings of the same situation, such as by drawing.

Sh, Sh, Sh

Out come the stars
Sh sh sh
Bright shines the moon
Sh sh sh
Sweet sings nightbird
Sh sh sh

"Go to bed
Sleepyhead"
Sandman said,
"Sh sh sh"

Listen

Listen to the noise
Listen to the noise
Listen to the noise
Made by those boys!

YOW!

Repetition often enhances a rhythm. In *Sh, Sh, Sh*, the repeated refrain can be used as a constant background beat or interspersed the way it is given. The refrain does give coherence to a change in rhythm and the movement in the narrative. In *Listen*, the repetition serves to build toward the climax of the last line. Voices will rise in volume until the last line is shouted.

Haiku

Pelicans at sea
Giant cups with wings
Fish peek out each side

Sky Ku

Skywriters' white streaks
Etch fine lines on azure
Writing P.S. I love you

More different shapes and rhythms in poems that will encourage children to explore the sounds to discover an appropriate rhythm. Both *Haiku* and *Sky Ku* can be extended into the areas of art and drama.

Around The Clock Talk

Block talk
Chalk talk
Crock talk
Dock talk
Clock talk
Jock talk
Gawk talk
Mock talk
Shock talk
Walk talk
Back talk
Flack talk
Small talk
Big talk
Rough talk
Tough talk
Smooth talk
Fast talk
Kid talk
Talk talk

TICK TOCK

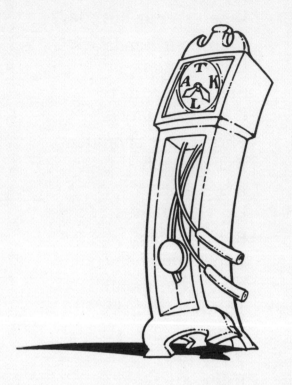

Playing with words is one of the keys to language learning. And what fun to learn how much you can do with one word. *Around The Clock Talk* uses the word ''talk'' to illustrate not only some rhyming words but words that seem to attach themselves naturally to it. ''Block'' and ''crock'' rhyme easily and ''small'' just belongs. ''Rough'' leads to ''tough'' and a whole new internal rhyme has happened. After a few lines of this chant are presented, participation by most children will follow.

The participation will likely produce different voices to convey the sense of the words. ''Rough'', ''tough'', ''smooth'', and ''fast'' will likely be spoken in different tones and speeds. You can integrate this or a similar chant into any number of class situations, or you could use it just for the sheer fun of playing with words.

Birthdays

Hey Hey
When's your Birthday?

Clap your hands
If it's January

Stamp your feet
If it's February

Shrug your shoulders
If it's March

If it's April
Up you stand

Born in May
Wave your hand

June's the month
To touch the sky

Fly around
If it's July

If it's August
Blow your nose

In September
Touch those toes

If your day is in October
Start that day
By rolling over

In November
Bend your knees

Here's December
You must freeze!

Birthdays has a powerful, strong beat; percussion can be added to heighten that beat. Children can be reminded that their own bodies are "beat-boxes". They can make their own sounds. This chant can be performed as a round, with birthday month children saying the lines that relate to that month. Alternately, everyone can repeat the chant, sitting or standing in a circle. Certainly, this is an active, physical education type of chant. It would be interesting to change the rhythm into a rap.

Brotherhood

Fly, fly, fly 'round the universe
Fly, fly, fly 'round the earth
Fly, fly, fly 'round the universe
Fly, fly, fly 'round the earth.

My feathers touch my brother.
My feathers touch my brother.
Circle, circle, circle, circle,
Circle to my brother.

Fly, fly, fly 'round the universe
Fly, fly, fly 'round the earth.

The rhythm is in the words of this chant. A traditional piece, it is excellent for drama and for movement. Children can be in a circle, holding hands for "my feathers touch my brother". It can be used as part of a cross cultural discussion to show how we are all connected with each other.

27

A Capella

Don't you know that you could do some singin'?
Without somebody violin-in'?
Without somebody playin' the drums?

Snap your fingers
Here it comes!

Clap your hands,
Stamp your feet
Shrug your shoulders
Shake your hips
Bend your knees
Swing and sway

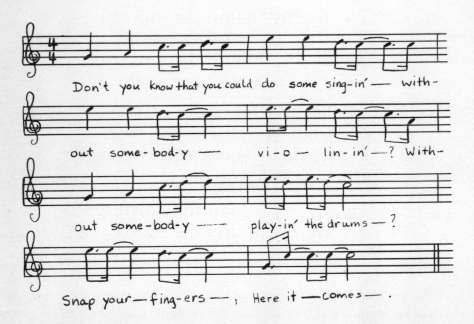

Music or a simple rhythmic beat can be added to most chants.
A suggested melody has been given for *A Capella*. Children will
"act out" the lines and can add more words and actions as they
go along.

Nonsense

Gooliba gooliba gooloon
A Snark flew up to the moon
And when he got there
He combed out his hair
And chanted a gooliba tune

Playing with words can also be done with made-up words as *Nonsense* illustrates. Euphonious words can be developed simply for the pleasure of putting the sounds together.

Coconut Warning

Now, here's a little warning
So listen to me
Never ever sit beneath
A coconut tree
They're great for drinking
They're fine for percussion
But if one hits your head
You'll get a concussion.

This chant is a rap — a rhythmic form familiar to most children.

Big Wide World

Big wide world
Big wide world

What shall we see in
The big wide world?

Shall we see a chicken
Peep, peep, peep?

Yes, we'll see a chicken
Peep, peep, peep.

Shall we see a duckling
Quack, quack, quack?

Yes, we'll see a duckling
Quack, quack, quack.

Shall we see a robin
Chirp, chirp, chirp?

Yes, we'll see a robin
Chirp, chirp, chirp.

Big wide world
Big wide world

What shall we see in
The big wide world?

Shall we see a . . .

Inspired by the National Film Board's production "Peep and the Big Wide World", this chant is a good example of a call and response form that develops its own rhythm from the way in which questions and answers are presented. Like most call and response or echo chants, it can be expanded by the children, and acted out in various ways. You can use other theme animals for variation such as farmyard animals, zoo animals, forest animals, jungle animals. For instance, "Shall we see a monkey? Chatter, chatter, chatter?"; "Shall we see a turtle? Go so slow.".

Things Puppets Can Do

A puppet in my pocket
A puppet in my hat
A puppet can do many things
Now, what do you think of that?

My puppet can say, "Yes Ma'm"
My puppet can say, "No!"
My puppet says, "That's yummy"
Or, "Sorry, I don't know."

My puppet walks quite slowly
And bows down very low
My puppet slides and runs fast
"Good-bye, It's time to go."

Using puppets can be a variation of call and response. The puppets can say the lines or do the actions. The children can ask the puppets the questions or help the puppets with their responses.

Puppets are an enormous help in the learning process. Playing with a puppet can overcome a child's reluctance to speak in front of the class; after all, it's the puppet that is doing the talking. A puppet can make any child more comfortable in the use of language.

Whenever you use a puppet, you should speak directly to the puppet, not to the group. An excellent resource is *The Instant Puppet Resourcebook for Teachers* by Lois and Herb Walker.

Rhythm and Rhyme

There's a rhythm in the air
There's a rhythm everywhere
There's a rhythm in the land
There's a rhythm in the band
There's a rhythm on the street
There's a rhythm in my feet
There's a rhythm in the stream
There's a rhythm in my dream
There's a rhythm in my walk
There's a rhythm in my talk
There's a rhythm in my toes
And it goes and goes and goes
There's a rhythm in the sea
There's a rhythm in ME!

Your Own Space

We can talk easily about the familiar things in our immediate environment. Children are no exception. The following collection of chants reflect some of my "familiars". The children will respond by producing chants and playlets that talk about people, animals, and situations close to them.

Holidays

Driving to the cottage
You can come too
Going to stay a week
For a Bar-B-Q
Fishing and
Swimming and
Surfing too
Looking for bears

                       and

A heron blue

No matter how children spend their holidays, they will understand the elements that could make up a holiday. Sometimes, a word or phrase will trigger an association in a child that goes in a different direction from what is being said. If this happens with this chant, let the children make up their own chant or rewrite this one. Whenever new material is generated by the children, it should be "printed" and available for others to read.

My Dog Jay

Ruggle dee
Buggle dee
My dog Jay
guards my house
both night and day
robbers, prowlers
stay away
You'll get scared
By my dog Jay

Mei Ling

She's a cranky old kitty
But I love her so
She spits and she hisses
When she steps in the snow
She can't stand children
'Cause they poke and they tease
"Don't bother me, baby,
I'm Siamese!"

Cat

My cat can stalk
My cat can walk
But how I wish
My cat could
        TALK!'

Special Diet

There's something wrong with Sasha
He doesn't want to purr
His motor isn't running
And all because of her

Her name is little Myshka
A teeny tiny mouse
She's peeking out at Sasha
Who can't get in her house

He's posted by her doorway
A hole where he won't fit
He doesn't want his dinner
And all he does is sit

The same old dried up cat food
Is all that's in the house
It isn't appetizing
When Sasha wants some "mouse"

Each class will have a variety of pets. Children may react to the warning in the dog chant or to the haughty conclusion of *Mei Ling* or the short story about what's bothering Sasha, but react they will, with tales of their own pets.

A discussion of those pets can be illustrated by a chart, showing the types and their names. Children should be encouraged to talk about why they like their pet, and how pets should be cared for. What do our pets do for us and what should we be doing for our pets? A writing assignment could be based on "what my dog or cat would say if it could talk."

In *Special Diet*, Myshka is a Ukrainian word for "little mouse".

Bad Mood Rap

When you come home from school
And you're in a bad mood
And your parents say,
"Come and eat your food."
And you don't feel hungry
And you don't feel nice
And the last thing you want
Is their advice
You just feel you want to
kick the cat
Or lie on your bed
in your favourite hat
Or stay in your room
and stare at the wall
And not talk to anyone at all
And if people call you
on the phone
You holler out loud, "Why don't you
leave me alone!"
You're as cross as a bear
and as mad as a snake
And you feel like cussin'
For goodness' sake

Well, hold on a minute
if you would
You're just in a very
frightful mood
So frightful you can almost cry
And, holy smoke,
You don't know why

Well, lots of times
we all feel like that
Feel like we want to kick the cat
And slam the door
On poor old Rover

But cheer up my friend
It'll soon be over

Let the children explore the rhythm of this rap, finding the right
"voice" to give meaning to words and phrases. Then the chant
can be done co-operatively with several people taking a couple
of lines each and joining together for the concluding two lines.

Loose Teeth

Brian lost his front tooth
In the strangest way
He was eating ice cream
After school one day
He bit down on a walnut
And then let out a roar
"Hey Mommy check this hole out
That wasn't there before!"

A fun chant that comments on that great experience of losing
teeth when you are young. New chants could be written about
other things we lose, such as "Lesley lost his ruler" or "Clara
lost her mittens".

Every Six Months

I went to the dentist
to get checked out
The dentist said, "Kelly,
open your mouth
You've brushed and flossed
after eating cheese.
That's why you have
            NO CAVITIES."

An easy way to introduce dental hygiene or to reinforce a lesson on teeth. Depending on the age range, a chart could be developed that showed how many teeth everyone has; the chart could also show how many wiggly teeth there are. The joyful shout of "No Cavities" is a good conclusion for one important part of tooth care. A chorus sound to imitate the sound of teeth brushing, such as "ch, ch, ch" could be added after every second line. Children can also mime flossing their teeth as they chant.

Babysitters

They never ask ME
If I'm allowed
That really makes me mad.
They always say, "Ask his parents!"
So they ask my Mom or Dad.
"Is HE allowed a piece of cake?
Is HE allowed T.V.
Is HE allowed to go outside
Or climb the apple tree
Is HE allowd to ride his bike
Or cross the road with Jed?"

But they never ask my parents
If I'm allowed to go to bed!

Children will enjoy finding the right "voices" for *Babysitters*. At
an early age they recognize that quotation marks mean dialogue,
a chance to use speaking voices.

Store Room

My own bedroom's
like a store
since I dumped
my dresser drawer
Piles of T shirts
on the floor
A hundred sox
or maybe more
I'm a salesman
I'm a clerk
Selling clothes is
quite hard work

Now I've changed
I'm buying pants
Show me some, please
for a dance
Have you any special shoes
A jumping pair
For me to choose?

Here comes Grandad
to my store
trying mittens
from the floor

Mommy's head peeks
'round my door
"PUT THOSE CLOTHES BACK
IN YOUR DRAWER!"

Katy

Katy Sticky Fingers
Smudges on the wall
Crumbs along the carpet
In the upstairs hall.

Everyone will recognize the familiarity of a messy room, and the dramatic possibilities of *Store Room* will add to the fun of this familiarity. The chant can be separated into seven parts with small groups of children chanting each part. The children might decide that a chorus of "messy, messy" or "trouble, trouble" would be an appropriate background. The first six groups could freeze into a tableau as Mommy chants, loudly, her lines. Props could easily be added but are not necessary; the children's imaginations can fill in all the blanks.

Katy could extend into a drawing or further verses using names of children in the class.

Practise Pain

Piano lessons
Piano lessons
Sitting on the stool
Piano lessons
Piano lessons
Practise after school
Piano lessons
Piano lessons
Practise every day

I don't want to practise
I JUST WANT TO PLAY.

Tennis Everyone

Upcourt
Downcourt
Sideways too
Forehand
Backhand
Lobby loo
Ace one
Place one
Don't disgrace one
Tennis is the game
for me and
for you.

Sports

Soccer in the morning
and in the afternoon
Playing for the A team
Gonna beat 'em soon

What do we do with our leisure time? Are there games we play with friends? Do we have things we have to do alone, like practising the piano lessons? No matter how you approach this group of chants, *Tennis Everyone* should be treated as a very active chant. A lot of movement should accompany the words. *Practise Pain* can have several "voices" in it, resignation through to indignation. *Sports* and *Tennis Everyone* can be treated as cheers, "Give me a T," etc.

Sharing

Now listen to my story
'Bout a not nice guy
He never shares his sandwich
or his apple pie
He keeps all his lunches
Safely hid
Man, he's some, mean,
stingy kid

Manners

Thank you
Please
Excuse me
You're welcome
If you please
Pardon me
Don't mention it
Magic words are these

Sharing and *Manners* are chants that allow two different entry points to a discussion of acceptable behaviours. You can talk about, and chant about, how to behave in a line-up waiting to go inside a movie theatre, riding a bicycle, eating lunch in the school cafeteria, going to the local variety store after school, working in the library, using playground equipment.

Name Nonsense

Sonja Sophie Serotiuk Dunn
Had so many names
They weighed a tonne
She put them in a sack
It was heavy as lead
Tied them with a string
And stored them under her bed.

Everyone enjoys making up rhyming words for their own names or their friends' names. Playing with words enables children to learn about language. Word awareness increases the knowledge of the sounds and rhythms of language.

All the chants that the children develop should be shared. Communication and thinking skills are enhanced by reading, writing, speaking, and drama — all elements that happen naturally in the sharing of chants.

Try making up chants using nicknames, such as ''Paul, Paul, Spinderball'' or ''Bubba, Bubba''.

Anti-Pollution Rap

Don't throw your garbage
Out on the street
Keep your planet
Clean and neat
Put your wrappers
In the big round bin
Recycle cans
That are made of tin
Take your bottles
Back to the store
Get a refund
To buy some more
Never toss junk
From a moving auto
'Cause "Clean is keen"
Should be your motto.

Today's children are very knowledgeable about pollution and its effects on the planet. They will be able to add suggestions to this rap. One suggestion to involve children in cleaning up their own room has been to make a garbage gobbling puppet. Such a puppet could be made by cutting in half the lid of a plastic container from ice cream or shortening. Paint stirring sticks can be glued to the inside of each half. A large paper bag can then be glued to the edges of the two halves. Hair, eyeballs, and a mouth can be added. The puppet is operated by moving the paint sticks to open the puppet's mouth and accept any garbage thrown in.

Children are exposed to world environment issues in their schools and through television programs such as those produced by David Suzuki. There are minimal ways in which they can effect changes globally, but children can be encouraged to do something about their immediate environment.

For Clara Evangeline

Sh sh quiet my dear
Sh sh sleepy time's here
May all your good wishes
And all your sweet dreams
Come true through the night
When the silver moon
beams

This chant is particularly good for primary school children just before their rest period. The children can be on the floor and help with the "Sh, sh, sh" for a few repetitions until everyone is quite still.

The following chant, developed by my son could also be used in this way:

Feed the baby
Wash the baby
Put the baby to bed
Wake the baby
Change the baby
Pat the baby's head

Paul Dunn

The gentle rhythm of the words can have a soothing effect. Alternatively, this chant could be used as a "wake-up call", with mimed actions to illustrate the words.

Different Days

Rainy rainy day
Rainy rainy day
We'll all get wet
On a rainy rainy day.

Sunny sunny day
Sunny sunny day
We'll all go swimming
On a sunny sunny day.

Snowy snowy day
Snowy snowy day
We'll all go sledding
On a snowy snowy day

Icy icy day
Icy icy day
We'll all go skating
On an icy icy day.

Frosty frosty day
Frosty frosty day
We'll freeze our noses
On a frosty frosty day.

This is a good chant for primary age children to do mime; the mime can be quite simple. Each verse can be taken by a small group and everyone joins in for the last line.

Be Prepared

Slippery
Sloppery
Slushery snow
Do up your snowshoes
And let's go.

Drippery
Droppery
Drizzery rain
Open your "yella" umbrella
Again

Mistery
Moistery
Mustery fog
Make sure you have
A strong leash for your dog.

The fun in this chant is from the sounds of the words. Sometimes they are "made-up" words but they are all onomatopoeic. The sound of the word is the sound of what is being described. This chant can lead to others using the principle of choosing words to imitate the sounds they represent. The better one can manipulate language, the better able one is to think, read, and write. Children should always be encouraged to use original and imaginative language.

Down in South Ontario

The moon needs a muffler in Moosonee;
stars need strings in Napanee;
the sun needs a shawl in cold Westree;
and I need mittens in Sudbury.

Trees need toques in Shining Tree;
the grass needs gloves in Atherley;
ponds need parkas in Sault Ste. Marie;
and I need earmuffs in Minaki.

But down in south Ontario,
the sun is always shining so
sometimes there's hardly any snow!
We shed our clothes and swimming go!

What marvellous drawings could be done to illustrate this chant!
A panel of drawings could be done with a separate illustration
for each verse. Or a three-dimensional panorama of the natural
scene could be constructed from papier-mâché using doll or baby
clothes to "dress" the trees, moon, etc. Or *Down in South Ontario*
could be treated as a rebus chant with pictures substituting for
certain words.

Shaking The Sillies

If the wind blows your umbrella
Completely inside out
Run between the raindrops
And shake your sillies out.

A chant can be only a few lines long yet still lead to good extensions. *Shaking the Sillies* could be a playlet or be shown in artwork.

Lotsa Winds

How many sounds
do the four winds make?

Hundreds and hundreds
for goodness' sake

Listen listen
to the sound
As they whoosh
around and 'round

Missssssssssssstral
SSSSSSSSSSSSSSSirroco
ChChChChChChChChChChinooooooook
Monssooooooooooooooooooooooon
Doldruuuuuuuuuuuuuuuuuum
Traaaaaaaaaaade wiiiiiiind
Northsouthwesteast wiiiiiiinds
ZZZZZZZZZZZZZZZZZZZephyr

If you make those sounds again
You may start a HURRICANE!

The weather really is a good topic to launch the possibilities of
enjoying language — different sounds, tempos, moods, and
vocabulary all happen.

Rainbow One

Please don't rush me Daddy
I want to taste the sun
I want to climb the rainbow
Now that the storm is done.

Rainbow Two

Rain goes
Rainbows!

Food Follies

Food appeals to everyone. And food conjures up particular tastes, sounds, emotions, and memories that are unique to each of us. Children enjoy words they can hear (crunch), taste (chocolate), see (rosy), touch (fuzzy), and smell (onion). Talking about food satisfies all those sensory needs. As well, children relate food to events and/or feelings. Maybe ice cream and popsicles are connected with a tonsilectomy, french fries with lunch out, turkey with holidays, popcorn with movies.

The following chants all have something to do with food. But each one takes a different "tack", uses a different voice and rhythm.

Turkey Time

Don't let the turkeys
Get you down
When they all come marching
Into your town
Look 'em in the eye
With a fearless frown
And roast 'em in the oven
'Till they're nice and brown

Turkeys are often associated with holiday times, particularly when you think of a great army of turkeys. However, this chant need not be restricted to a holiday time such as Thanksgiving. Teachers in one of my workshops helped me work out *Turkey Time*.

A Mess To Eat

A marshmallow
Fell on my shirt
It looked like
A patch
Of white dirt
My shirt was all messy
So what could I do?
I ate it right up
For dessert.

The things that happen to children — and adults too. Ask the children to turn this little chant into a limerick form.

Canadian Tomatoes

You can eat a red tomato
On the coast of Spain
Or on a beach in Florida
Or in Bahrain
You can gulp one down
In Africa
North south east west
But Canadian tomatoes
Taste the very best!
    YEA TOMATOES!

This rap about *Canadian Tomatoes* is heartfelt; I really do think our tomatoes taste the best. Children may have similar feelings about another food, and can develop a cheer for it.

Rise 'n Shine

You gotta rise and shine
in the morning
You gotta rise and shine
at noon
Rise and Shine
Rise and Shine
Suppertime will be here soon

You gotta rise and shine
at breakfast
You gotta rise and shine
at lunch
Rise and Shine
Rise and Shine
Everybody in a bunch

This is an action chant that uses the whole body. Finger-snapping, hand-clapping, jumping up on the last line of each verse can also be accompanied by the group "making waves" with their bodies.

Sky High

Beam me up
Up so high
Beam me higher
To the sky

Beam me down
Tout de suite
Mom's got lunch
For me to eat

Children's imaginations will soar as they design chants of their own that associate foods with space. Here is another space chant I developed:

Would you go into orbit
If you were invited
And fly in space
With lunch provided?
Would you eat a dry diet
Of astronaut glop
And give up your favourite
Pizza and pop?

Drinks

Bergy seltzer
Fizzy popper
A big loada soda is a
thirst stopper

A nonsense rhyme that encourages children to use different sounds to achieve an effect. Dr. Zed (Gordon Penrose) told me that bergy seltzers were made from ice bergs — imagine!

In A Labrador Eatery

There's something fishy in Labrador
They're serving up cods' tongue
And everyone is eating it
The old and very young.

There's Kenamu salmon
Hot Mulligan Scoff
Some codfish o'grattin
And if that's not enough
Try In the Tilt Grub
It's cooked for the tough.

Labrador menu
Is very good stuff.

In Barry and Eric Barricks restaurant in Lake Melville, Labrador,
I was intrigued with the items on the menu and their descrip-
tions. This chant happened from that experience.

To "scoff" is to eat a big meal; "o grattin" is really "au gratin"
or "with cheese"; a "tilt" is a trapper's little cabin. Collo-
quialisms, local expressions, slang can all be used in chants to
add to the sound patterns or to make a story belong to a particular setting.

Double Whammy

Pizza and pop
Pizza and pop
When I get started
I just can't stop
The smell is delicious
The taste extra yummy
I love it the most
When it gets to my tummy

A basic rhyming scheme, the same one as was used in *Crackers and Crumbs* keeps *Double Whammy* rolling along. Try this cheerleading type of rhythm with "burgers and fries", "hot dogs and chips" or "candy and gum" — or have children develop their own combination.

Another good rhythm for a cheer chant was developed by my son Paul in the following chant.

Popsicles
Popsicles
Taste so sweet
Popsicles
Popsicles
Hard to beat
Whenever the weather
Is sunny and hot
Popsicles
Popsicles
Eat 'em a lot
Lickety
Lickety
Lickety
Lick
'Till all
That is left
Is a
Popsicle stick!

© Paul Dunn

Who'd Have Thought-on?

Susan Cotton
Lives in Naughton
She will never be forgotten
She picks apples
When they're rotten
Puts them in a big hot pot 'n
Makes sweet cider
Nice and hot 'n

Another good chance to play with words, this chant is based on a real person. Suzanne Cotton does live in Naughton on the Trans Canada highway in northern Ontario. She does have an orchard but she doesn't use rotten apples for her cider — poetic license on my part!

Tonions of Onions

Tonions of onions
for us to eat
Tonions of onions
around our feet
Tonions of onions
a scrumptious treat
They fell from a truck
That turned onto our street

I actually saw this happen; a truck lost its load of onions and they were rolling all over the street. I am sure that the children will remember equally absurd scenes that they have witnessed with food, such as someone pulling out one squash from a super-market counter and dislodging more.

Good "Eats"

Cookies in the car
Cookies in the car
Somebody stole them
From the cookie jar
Crumbs on the dashboard
Crumbs on the seat
Cookies taste the best
And are the best to eat.

A Fable For Everyone

The Magical Tree

The animals were thirsty
But there was no rain
They were hungry
In the forest
And were filled
With pain
The land was dry and dusty
All the trees
Had died
The riverbeds were cracked
And the earth
Was fried.

"Oh dear, oh dear
What shall we do?"
Cried the hungry kangaroo.

"If we don't band together,"
The old turtle said,
"We'll wander on forever
Till our tribe is dead!"

So they joined
In a team
As they travelled on
When all of a sudden
There appeared a lawn.

On that grass
Grew a lush green tree
Loaded with fruit
That was hanging free.

"This fruit's for you
This fruit's for me!"
Cheered all the animals
Happily.

"It smells delicious
This succulent fruit
And there's tonnes and tonnes
Of it, to boot!"

It looked like
Apples
Oranges
Grapes

Bananas
Pears and
Pomegranates.

It only took a minute
For every beast
To put on a bib
For this splendid feast.

It smelled like mangoes
Apricots
Peaches
But when they tried
To pluck some
It eluded their reaches.

No matter how hard
The animals tried
The fruit just waved
From side to side.

They couldn't grasp it
In their paws
They couldn't bite it
With their jaws.

"Oh dear, oh dear
What shall we do?"
Cried the hungry kangaroo.

Said the wise old owl
"I just might know;
I heard of this tree
A long time ago
From my Grandmother
A wise old dame.
She said this tree
Had a special name
And if we guess
The name of this tree
It will give
Its fruit
To you and me."

Owl said, "Whooooooo
Could guess this thing?"
Cheetah suggested,
"Let's find the King."

But the King was very occupied
Deep in the woods
With his brand new bride.

King Lion lived far
Across the plain
Beside the hill
On Royalty Lane.

So the animals
Went to their
Lion King
That big cat knew
'Most everything.

And they said
"Your Grace
We're dying of thirst
Things are going
From bad to worse
We fear our tribe
Will soon disperse."

"You're wise, dear subjects,
To come to me
The name you seek is
The Koolibah tree."

"Thank you, Your highness
We bow at your feet."

Then the band returned
On sure swift feet.
They chanted this song
And prepared to eat.

"Koolibah Koolibah Koolibah tree
Bend your branches
Down to me.

Koolibah Koolibah Koolibah tree
Bend your branches
Down to me."

The big tree swayed
And leaned down low
The marvellous fruit
Stopped moving so.

And pick the fruit
The animals could
They ate and ate
For it tasted good.
Good like the fruit
Of a Koolibah should.

They chanted and sang
On bended knee,
"Thank you thank you
Koolibah tree."

From that day on
That magic tree
Provided fruit
For all to see
And everytime
A piece was picked
The tree replaced
The fruit
Quite quick.

Delicious food
That kind tree bore
The animals hungered
Nevermore!

There are infinite possibilities for the presentation of this chant. One good starting point could be to have an older class develop it as a presentation to younger grades. The younger ones will feel honoured to be an audience for a special presentation, and the older ones will enjoy sharing the "fruits of their labour" (no pun intended). In fact, the concept of sharing between classes is always something to be encouraged because it usually has such positive consequences.

First, parts should be assigned for the kangaroo, turtle, owl, cheetah, and King Lion. Depending on the size of the group, these parts can be taken by one student or several. Decisions should be made about what actions might accompany the group speeches. Are the group speeches to be given by everyone or should there be a narrator who provides the story line?

Everyone must grapple with the various changes in rhythm within the chant, and decide which is most appropriate. Almost instinctively, they will know that they have to change voice as they go along. If they use a high pitch in their voice, it will denote excitement, happiness, exhileration. If they use a low pitch, they will reflect feelings of sadness, worry, or even mystery. When they use a high pitch, they will likely speak more quickly. The pitch of the voice that is used is needed as a clue to the listeners to alert them to what is coming, what they can expect to happen.

A variety of voices is important in any dramatic presentation. Pauses and the way phrases are linked are also very important. These are some of the principles of choral speaking.

In choral speaking, children are responding as a group which is sometimes less inhibiting than solo oral presentations. Articulation is essential when a group is speaking.

Reading aloud, which is the beginning of presenting such a chant, can stimulate learning. Children discover how to manipulate a text. Their eyes and ears are trained to explore language rhythms, and they are encouraged to try new sounds and patterns.

The Magical Tree can be presented purely orally and be a delight. If the class is so inclined, imaginative props can be added. Music could certainly be introduced, from simple percussion to more elaborate accompaniment. Drawings or paintings could be done to reflect the chant's content. Certainly, *The Magical Tree* is perfect for a readers' theatre. Children "on stage" can step forward to say their lines. Additionally, children can stand on benches or boxes to present different heights that will add to the effectiveness of their reading.

Other fables could be introduced and discussed; try using some from different cultures. Ask students to design a chant based on the story line of another fable. Celia Barker Lottridge's *The Name of the Tree*, can be a wonderful introduction or follow-up to this traditional, international folk tale. Or develop a chant from such tales as ''The Three Little Pigs'', ''The Three Sillies'', ''Stone Soup'', ''The Golden Fish'', ''Why The Elephant Has A Long Trunk'', ''How the Leopard Got Its Spots''.

Fantasy and Fun

The world of imagination and make-believe may have been weakened for today's children who are exposed to so many visual images, BUT it has not become obsolete. Children still delight in imagining the scary, the absurd, and the fanciful.

Boo!

The boogey man
The boogey man
Came to town
Scared all the kids
For miles around
He booed in the night
And he made them squeal
But they laughed at his BOO
'Cause they knew he wasn't real!

This chant should be introduced by a conversation about what is real and what is make-believe so that the children can be frightened only in play.

Balderdash

Niddy-noddy	Balderdash
Kohlrabi	Balderdash
Gourami	Balderdash
Kiyoodle	Balderdash
Collywobbles	Balderdash
Aggerwator	Balderdash
Clewgarnet	Balderdash
Charivari	Balderdash
Rowlyrag	Balderdash
Koradgee	Balderdash
Humdudgeon	Balderdash
Morpunkee	Balderdash
Hogmanay	Balderdash

Play the game of Balderdash
Give yourself a nervous rash

These may look like nonsense words but, believe it or not, they are all real. You can use a dictionary and find some other unusual words to add to this call and response chant. Try words like ''contango'', ''habnab'', ''cuscus'', ''furuncle'', or make up your own words.

Sauruses

Mommysaurus
Daddysaurus
Babysaurus too
Went for a walk
To the city zoo
They growled at the tigers
They yelled at the yaks
They squealed at the elephants
And jumped upon their backs
They drank popsaurus
They ate saurusteaks
They gobbled junkosaurus food
And went home with tummy aches

Making up nonsense words and using them in poetry or rapping can be challenging. Sometimes, my whole family joins in and says absurd things. My son, Kevin, once said, "Do we always have to talk in Chaucerian rhymes in this house?"

Who's A Scaredy Cat?

I never met a dragon
That I didn't like
Especially a dragon
Riding on a trike

I never met a tiger
That I didn't pet
Especially a tiger
Whose nose was cool and wet

I never met a bunyip
At whom I didn't wave
Especially while walking
Past a darkened cave

I never met a dinosaur
At whom I didn't smile
Especially a dinosaur
Closer than a mile.

It's easy to be brave when you're at a zoo and see some large animals, but how would you feel if you were really close to these "creatures"? Ask the children to develop a poem that opens with, "If I met a dragon. . .".

Don't Question A Giant

Hey there Giant
Where do you walk?
> Up and around
> The tall beanstalk.

Hey there Giant
What do you eat?
> Grims and grums
> And platypus' feet.

Hey there Giant
What do you say?
> I'll have *you* for lunch
> another day.

This is another example of a question and answer, call and response chant that can be enjoyed by any age group. The group can be divided into Giants and Questioners, and can make up more questions and answers.

Push Button Baby

Let me tell you 'bout a boy
He's his mother's son
He's a button pusher
That's how he gets his fun

Chorus: He's a push button baby,
     push button baby,
   He's a push button baby
   Pushing buttons all day long

He gets so excited when
The microwave goes beep
He turns his tape recorder on
To rock him off to sleep

If he can't find a button
At least there is a dial
That should keep him happy
For a little while

He thinks you press a button
To raise the morning sun
He's thoroughly convinced
And he wants to see it done

He knows a button raises
The windows on the car
But which one would he press
To see the moon and stars?

© Paul Dunn

Let me tell you 'bout a boy, He's his moth-er's son,

He's a but-ton push-er, And that's how he gets his fun, He's a

push but-ton ba-by ——— , He's a

push but-ton ba-by ————————— , He's a

push but-ton ba-by ——— , Push-in' but-tons all day— long——— .

Automation is no longer fantastical but this chant written by my
son Paul shows that there can still be some fun and fantasy
attached to a ''computer kid''. The chorus can be repeated after
each verse or can provide the background beat. Suggested music
has been given for *Push Button Baby*.

Justin John

Justin John
Justin John
Where were you
While I was gone?
I was walking on the lawn
One shoe off and
One shoe on

This chant, sounding as though it is connected to a somewhat familiar nursery rhyme, is actually based on the name of the person. Justin John had such a musical quality to it that it almost demanded a chant be composed around the name. Justin John was a junior kindergarten student of my son, Kevin, when he was principal of the Beedaban School in Massey, Ontario. The day I visited the school, Justin John came to school, wearing just one shoe — he must have lost it along the way.

Superstition

Timothy Eaton's splendiferous toe
Just in case you didn't know
Will bring you good luck
It never can miss
If you pucker your lips
and give it a kiss.

In fact, the superstition about the statute of Timothy Eaton, that has been incorporated into Toronto's Eaton Centre, is that you rub his toe — but doesn't this make a better conclusion? See what superstitions the children can work into chant form.

Pirates Bold

Pirates bold
In days of old
Sailing o'er the seas
Jolly Roger
Flying high
"Pass the silver, please!"

A pictorial depiction of this chant could lead to several interpretations. Are the pirates showing each other their bounty or are they dining in fine style with silver, china, and crystal? All interpretations or variations are acceptable; there are no right answers to the meaning. Sometimes, asking questions is more important than finding the answers.

Longa Legga

Momma longa legga
Uh uh uh
Momma longa legga
Uh uh uh
Momma longa legga
Walk walk walk
Momma longa legga
Walk the walk

Daddy longa legga
Uh uh uh
Daddy longa legga
Uh uh uh
Daddy longa legga
Stalk stalk stalk
Daddy longa legga
Stalk the walk

Sister longa legga
Uh uh uh
Sister longa legga
Uh uh uh
Sister longa legga
Talk talk talk
Sister longa legga
Talk the walk

Brother longa legga
Uh uh uh
Brother longa legga
Uh uh uh

Brother longa legga
Chalk chalk chalk
Brother longa legga
Chalk the walk

Baby longa legga
Sh sh sh
Baby longa legga
Sh sh sh
Baby longa legga
She NO TALK

This chant has been included under Fantasy and Fun because it is so much fun for a group of children to do. The words lead easily to a train, a chain, a join-on, a conga line. I know that my grandchildren, Kaitlin (2) and Brian (6) love doing a conga in the living room when life gets a little boring after dinner.

The repetition in the chant encourages participation. An adjunct to this positive element of repetition is that, by repetition, children are able to develop a sense of ownership over language and its patterns. Such ownership is reinforced by speaking, pictorializing, dramatizing, and writing.

My Story Hat

I've got a hat
That I love to wear
Every day
Every day
Of the year
It's all smashed up
And it has a tear
But that makes it better
My dear
There's a stain on the brim
But to me it looks trim
And it has a few things
Tied on it
Like crossbones and skulls
And spiders and gulls
It's my favourite story bonnet

This chant is in praise of my story hat. I have found that both my story hat and my story skirt have fantasy and fun in them for children. As someone who works and plays with children, you might find such devices useful. The items you choose to include on these pieces of clothing can be triggers for a particular story, can supplement a tale, or just add a little surprise.

Favourites

Have you got a hat
That you love to wear?
A hat that you take
Most everywhere?
You wear it to school
You wear it to bed
You never ever
Take it
Off your head
You wear it to play
And to do your math
But your mom
Won't let you wear it
When you take a bath.

A "springboard" chant that happened when I started to
think about other people's hats.

Puppets Alive

A puppet in my pocket
A puppet on my hat
A puppet in my storyskirt
Now what do you think of that?
A puppet bows, "Good morning"
A puppet says "I'm shy."
A puppet says "I'm hungry."
A puppet waves Goodbye.

All the wonderful things that can be facilitated by puppets can be demonstrated with a simple chant such as this. Teaching English as a second language can be helped by the use of puppets. Children with different abilities can be encouraged to speak through puppets. In any "first time" situations, puppets can break down barriers by asking informational questions of individuals — who could be shy when a puppet is asking the questions? Children will respond to the actions as well as the words of a puppet. Try it!

Rabbit Reading Rap

Now Jack let me tell you
Why I hate to read
'Cause the people all worry
I got no speed
Rapid they say
Rapid's the way
But I never heard a rabbit
Read to this day

Remember that a rap always has an accompanying beat, even if it is only finger-snapping or thigh-slapping. Who knows, someone might even decide to breakdance to this one! Watch for the play on words; your audience may think you're saying ''rabbit'' rather than ''rapid''.

Down Under

Wallabies on waterskis
Watch those babies bend their knees
Pouches floating in the breeze
They're Australian,
If you please!

Try making new chants using phrases such as "wolverines on trampolines".

Special Times

Special times are always good excuses to make up chants. I give you a few of my favourites in this section, but I know you and the children around you will develop many more.

Valentine One

Hearts and flowers
And a valentine
Tell me honey
That you'll be mine.

Valentine Two

One two I love you
Three four I did before
Five six We could mix
Seven eight Be my mate
Nine Ten In love again.

Valentine's Day is one of the easiest special times on which to make up rhyming chants. It seems all the words one associates with this time rhyme.

Perfect Night

A perfect night for lizards
A perfect night for bats
A perfect night for goblins
A perfect night for cats
A perfect night for witches
Who haunt and spook the night
A perfect night for Hallowe'en
PLEASE DON'T TURN OUT THE LIGHT!

Ghosties

Goblins and ghosts
Goblins and ghosts
On Hallowe'en
They ate up my toast
They ate up my jam
They ate up my pears
Then jumped into their beds
At the top of the stairs.

Hallowe'en Dress-Up

Each Hallowe'en I have an itch
To dress up like a wicked witch
To don my big black pointed hat
Wake my "familiar", Boris bat
Dust off my broom of sassafras
Slip on my cloak of fashion class
Have my black wig completely curled
Then, with Feline, go spook the world.

As anyone who knows me will verify, Hallowe'en is one of my favourite "special times". I love getting dressed up! So do lots of other kids! It's no wonder I'm often called "Mrs. Make-Believe".

Perfect Night should be read with a rising inflection of voices until the last line becomes almost a screech. *Ghosties* has the same rhythm as *Crackers and Crumbs*. *Hallowe'en Dress-Up* is a more sophisticated chant; older children will relate to the humour in the lines and discover what a "familiar" might be (a lizard, black cat, owl, bat, etc.).

Chantski

The snow gets deep
and the wind gets cold
The cars just slide
'cause the wheels won't roll

But this big storm
just can't stop me
I'm going to school
'cause I've got my skis

Chorus: Slide, slide, slide on the ice
Slide, slide, slide on the snow
Slide, slide, slide on the ice
There's no place that I can't go

I've got my poles
I've got my boots
I look great in
my new ski suit

The snow comes up
to people's knees
But I don't sink
'cause I've got my skis

Chorus: Slide, slide, slide on the ice
Slide, slide, slide on the snow
Slide, slide, slide on the ice
There's no place that I can't go

The outside world
slows to a crawl
But kids like me
don't care at all

In less than the time
it takes to sneeze
I'll get there
on my brand new skis

Chorus: Slide, slide, slide on the ice
Slide, slide, slide on the snow
Slide, slide, slide on the ice
There's no place that I can't go

© Paul Dunn

The chorus can be accompanied by appropriate movements. This cheerful chant can be used in the new year after the first snow has fallen, and after new skis may have been a gift.

Ho, Ho, Ho

What does Santa say
As he flies through the snow?
Merry merry Christmas
HO HO HO

What does Santa say
To make his reindeer go?
Merry merry Christmas
HO HO HO

Jingle Bell Moose

What would you do
If the Jingle Bell Moose
Landed on your lawn
When he got loose
From Santa's sleigh
On Christmas Eve?
Would you ask him to stay
Or ask him to leave?
Would you give him some cookies
And a pail of juice
Then take him to the dentist
For his tooth that's loose?

For some children, Christmas is also a special time. These chants provide two ways to introduce the holiday season — one traditional and one with a little humour.

Places To Be

Many of our place names, street names, waterway names, town names have a rhythmical quality all their own. They lend themselves to verse quite easily. The following chants give a sample of what you can do using different formats.

Joggling

Joggle up Yonge Street
Joggle all day
Joggle joggle joggle
It's a long long way
Joggle past Trout Creek
And Temagami
Does Yonge Street go to
Moosonee?

Joggling and *Meetings*, on the next page use names that are common to many North American communities. Children will enjoy making up verses for their own community.

Meetings

I met a man on Main Street
In the town of Burnaby
He bowed and said, "Good morning,"
And asked me in for tea.

I met a girl on Queen Street
In the town of Moosonee
She gave me some red berries
From a small red berry tree.

I met a boy on King Street
In the town of Come By Chance
He had his ghetto blaster
And asked me for a dance.

I met some friends on Front Street
In the town of Barrys Bay
We stood on a street corner
And rapped away all day.

Index